Start Right Reader

GRADE 2 · BOOK 6

Printed in the U.S.A.

ISBN 978-1-328-82597-1

9 10 0928 26 25 24 23 22

4500843702 B C D E F G

Contents

MODULE 12

Week 1

Week 2

Week 3

Get Started

Nan and Pop are staying with Alex, Vincent, and their dad, or papa, while their mom is away. Nan and Pop tell the boys a story about when their papa was a boy.

What happened when Papa tried to ride a pony? Was it as wild a ride as Papa claims? Read to find out!

Vincent

Alex

Nan

Pop

Mama

Papa

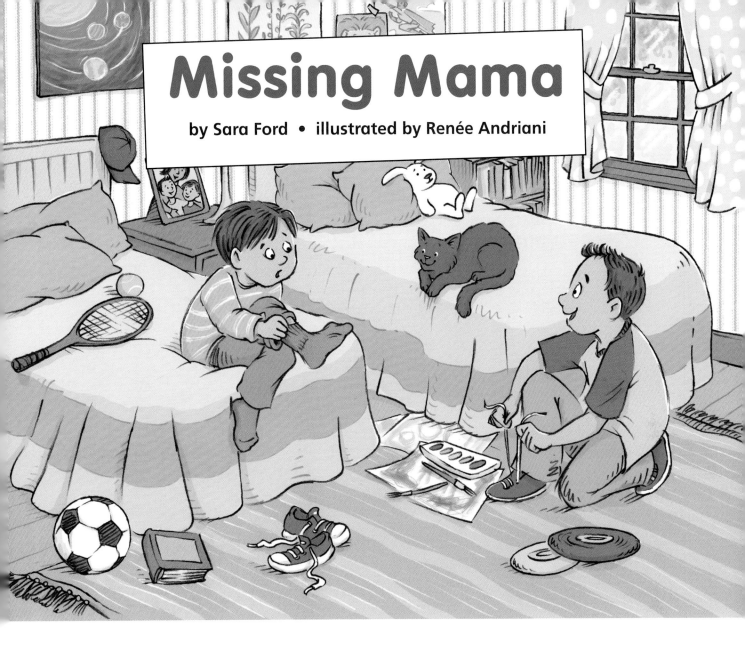

Missing Mama

by Sara Ford • illustrated by Renée Andriani

"When will Mama come home?" Vincent asked his big brother, Alex. "It's taking too many days for Julie to get better."

"No, Mama left just two days ago," said Alex. "But you're right, it feels longer. I miss her, too."

Mama had gone to help her sister, Julie. Julie fell off her bike and broke her arm. Her broken arm was in a cast. It was hard for her to do some things with her arm in a cast.

While Mama was with her sister, Nan and
Pop were staying with them to help their papa.
Alex and Vincent headed for the kitchen. Pop
had cooked a surprise for them—pancakes!

"I've got another surprise for you," Pop said.
"When your papa gets home from work, we will
all go visit your mama and Julie."

"Yay!" Vincent shouted.

"I'm happy, too," Nan said, smiling widely.

"Did you ever have a broken arm?" Alex asked Nan and Pop.

"No, not me," Pop replied, "but your papa nearly broke his arm when he was a boy."

"He was ten years old," added Nan.

"What happened?" Alex asked.

Pop and Nan looked at each other and started to chuckle. Vincent stopped eating. He was eager to hear this story.

"Well," began Pop, "we had a friend who had a nice old pony named Peanut. She told your papa that he could take a ride on Peanut."

Nan picked up the story. "Your papa told his friends that Peanut was a wild, speedy horse," said Nan. "But Peanut was just the sweetest, most gentle old pony. Your papa strutted up to Peanut like a cowboy on TV."

"Then what happened?" Vincent asked.

"Your papa climbed up on the left side of Peanut," Pop said, "but instead of sitting in the saddle, he sailed right across it!"

"He landed on the other side of Peanut, and quite suddenly he was sitting on the ground instead of on a pony," Nan said. "It was too bad about that puddle he landed in," Nan added. "He ended up on the ground and soaking wet."

"I will never forget the look of complete surprise on his face!" said Pop, laughing.

"That's funny," said Alex.

"Tell it again!" cried Vincent.

"Later, boys," said Nan. "It's time for you to get to school. Grab your things and let's go."

"I can't wait until Papa gets home and we can go see Mama," Vincent told Alex.

Story Word Tally

Make a list of the words below.

mama	sister	home	happy	happened
papa	brother	help	surprise	suddenly

1. Look for each word in the story. Make a tally mark each time you find a word.

2. Compare lists with a partner. Do your tallies match?

3. Take turns with your partner. Use each word in a sentence.

Blend and Read

1. neatly   unsteady   remained   painfully

2. weekly   seesaw   outgrow   showy

3. chatted   shipping   chipped   pitching

4. carpet   mislabeled   gardening   disease

5. steerage   preseason   unreachable   unveiling

6. Vincent is eager to hear the story Pop tells.

7. Papa will ride the subway with the boys today.

8. When Papa was ten, he fell off Peanut.

Papa Tells His Side

by Sara Ford • illustrated by Renée Andriani

Finally, the afternoon ended, and Papa came home from work. It was time to go see Mama and Julie.

"We'll take the subway across town," said Nan, "and then walk the rest of the way."

"Are we going to the clinic?" Vincent asked.

"No," said Papa. "Mama is with Julie at her house. We will visit them at home."

"Papa, I am used to going on the subway with Mama," Vincent said. "It's funny having you here on the train with us!"

"It's a good thing you didn't fall out of the other side of the train when you got in, Papa," Alex said with a grin.

Papa looked surprised. "What do you mean?" he asked.

"I have never fallen out the other side of anything!" Papa exclaimed. "How could you say that?" He winked at Alex.

"That's not what Pop told us!" Vincent yelled.

"You must be referring to my wild ride on that bucking bronco when I was ten," said Papa.

"That's not what we heard!" said Alex. "We heard it was a pony named Peanut, and he never moved an inch."

"Yes, now I remember," said Papa. "I got up on old Peanut very carefully, but suddenly he leaped into the air and I fell off."

Vincent flopped over sideways onto Papa and giggled into his hands.

"Tell it right, Papa!" he insisted.

Papa laughed. "All right, all right," he said. "I agree with the story you heard. It's true. I fell off a pony that was standing as still as stone."

Alex nudged his little brother. "Look, Vincent," he said. "We're here. This is the stop."

When they got to the right block, Mama came downstairs to meet them. Vincent flung his arms around her. She hugged her boys tight.

"We miss you so much," said Alex.

"I miss you, too, sweetie," said Mama. "But I'll be home soon. My sister is doing really well and won't need as much help from me."

The smell of blueberry coffeecake greeted
them as they entered the house.

"What a nice surprise!" Julie cried. "I'm
so happy to see you. Thanks for letting your
mama stay and help me." She showed the boys
her cast. "You can write on it," she said. Alex
wrote, "Your bike is like a pony. Ask Papa!"

"I've got to hear this!" Julie said. "What
happened? How can my bike be like a pony?"

Think-Pair-Share

Reread both stories. Think about your answers to the questions below.

1. Why is Pop's story about Papa funny? Use details from the story in your answer.

2. Why does Papa tell the story differently than Pop tells it?

3. What does Alex write on Julie's cast? Why?

Think and then talk with a partner. Then share your ideas with a group.

Get Started

What do you know about Earth? What is the weather like where you live? What is the weather like in faraway places on Earth?

How do plants and animals survive where they live? Can they survive anywhere, or do they need to live in certain places? Read to find out!

Earth

by Christina Wilsdon

The planet we live on is called Earth. It is the third planet away from the sun. Water covers much of the planet and surrounds all the land.

Look at a globe to see if you can find your country. Is it near the sea? Some countries are quite close to the sea, while others are far away from the sea. Countries that do not border a sea do not have a coast.

The top and bottom of Earth are called its **poles**. The North Pole is at one end, and it is freezing cold all year long. Large sheets of ice and ice chunks float on its cold sea.

It is so cold at the North Pole because the sun is always fairly low in the sky. The sunlight is too weak to warm the sea very much or melt all its ice. For these same reasons, the South Pole at the other end of Earth is freezing cold, too.

Around the middle of Earth is a zone that is always warm. This zone is called the tropics.

Jungles in the tropics are filled with tall trees, strong vines, and lush ferns. Jungles in the tropics are hot, green, steamy places that get rain each day. Grasslands in the tropics, however, may get lots of rain at one time. Then the weather is mostly dry for the rest of the year. Then the rains return, and the pattern repeats.

Places that fall between the tropics and the poles have weather that changes during the year. These places have more seasons than places near the poles or the tropics.

One country in these parts of the planet might have hot summers and cold winters with lots of snow. Another country in these parts might have warm summers and chilly winters with hardly any snow at all.

If you live near the sea, you might enjoy a summer that is cooler than summer in a place that is farther from the sea. In daytime, you will get the cool breezes that blow off the water and onto the land.

In the middle of a big country, summer may be quite long and hot. Summers like this are good for growing crops. Farmers plant corn and wheat, and before long they can harvest them.

   Plants that can grow in wet places might not grow well in dry places that get little rain. Likewise, plants that do well in dry places might not thrive, or even survive, in wetter, rainy lands.

   This is true for other living things, too. This bird, for example, can't survive in snowy places because it can't stay warm or find the food that it prefers to eat. Its home is a forest in the tropics that is hot, wet, steamy, and green.

Letter Mix-Up

Read the words below to a partner.

away	because	plant	rain	else
green	country	earth	sea	sun

Oh, no! The letters in the words got mixed up! Work with your partner. Write the letters in order to spell a word in the box.

1. i n a r

2. s l e e

3. e r g n e

4. l n p a t

5. a b c e e s u

6. u n s

7. y w a a

8. a h t r e

9. a s e

10. u c t o n y r

Blend and Read

1. farming   farmer   restart   disturb   return

2. tearful   fearless   thirsty   careful   birthday

3. coating   bowling   greedy   neatly   opening

4. weighty   eighty   prey   sleigh   they

5. alligator   helicopter   caterpillar

6. The rainforest is home to colorful butterflies.

7. Are summers and winters cold at the poles?

8. A country in the tropics is warm all year.

Life on Earth

by Christina Wilsdon

A rainforest is hot and wet. Rain falls each day. Water drips from green leafy branches and bright flowering plants. Butterflies flutter by. It is the perfect home for this pretty bird.

With its big bill, this bird eats sweet morsels and nabs insects, frogs, and eggs to eat. It must live in a rainforest, or else it could not find the food it needs. It would not survive on a cold mountain or in a desert with few trees or plants.

This bird, however, could not live in a rainforest. It cannot fly or perch in a tree. It needs to live in the cold, snowy places near the South Pole of Earth.

This kind of bird has fluffy feathers close to its skin that keep it warm. Its outer feathers are flat and stiff. When it dives into icy seas to catch fish to eat, those outer feathers form a waterproof covering.

This hare lives in a cold, snowy place, too.
It is called an Arctic hare. It lives in Arctic lands,
the lands that circle the North Pole.

An Arctic hare has thick fur to keep it warm.
Its color is white or blue-gray, so it can seem to
vanish in the snow. It tries to stay hidden, or
else it might be discovered by a snowy owl,
fox, or hawk out hunting for food.

This kind of hare lives far from the Arctic in a hot, dry desert. Its tan and black fur blends in with the dirt and sand of its desert home.

Its ears are much bigger than the ears of an Arctic hare. These big ears help keep it cool. Breezes blow across the thin skin on the big ears. The air whisks away body heat and helps cool the hare.

This fox lives in a desert, too. Like the hare, it has big ears that help it keep cool. It gets much of the water it needs from its food, so it doesn't need to make so many stops at waterholes.

It is very good at burrowing. It spends its days in its cool burrow away from the hot sun and does its hunting at night. Because of its thick fur, it is warm in the chilly darkness. The fuzz on its paws helps it scamper over the sand.

An Arctic fox has fuzzy feet, but its fuzz is for walking on snow, not sand. The fuzz keeps its feet warm and helps it grip onto ice and snow. It has small ears tucked into a thick, furry coat.

In summer, its fur darkens until it blends in with the dirt and rocks. In winter, it turns white or blue-gray to blend in with the snow. This hardy fox can curl up to take a cozy nap in snowstorms, surrounded by its warm, furry tail.

Show What You Know

Reread both texts to answer the questions.

1. Choose two places that you read about.
    Describe the weather in both places.
    How is the weather the same? How is the
    weather different?

2. Choose an animal that you read about.
    How does it survive where it lives?

Talk about your answers with a partner.

Personal Response

Which kind of place on Earth is a place where
you would like to live? Why would you like to
live there?

Share your ideas with a partner or in a group.

Get Started

Drake, Mom, and Dad live on Planet Nine. They are planning a party for their extended family, but they have a big problem!

What is the problem? Will Drake, Mom, and Dad be able to resolve it in time for their party? Read to find out!

Drake

Mom

Dad

A Big Problem

by Bryan Langdo • illustrated by Karl West

Drake and his family lived in a roomy burrow beside a hill on Planet Nine. It was a remote planet. Drake rarely saw his uncles and other family members since they lived so far away.

So he felt very happy when Mom said, "We will invite the family to a big party. It's too long since we've seen them. They can sleep here and stay with us as long as they like."

For weeks, Drake helped his mom and dad get ready for the huge party. At last, it was the day before the big event.

"People will get here early tomorrow," Dad said. "At least twenty people say they will be sleeping over. I wish they had told me sooner. We'll need a bed for each one of them!"

Dad began to pace back and forth.

"Wow," said Drake. "That will be quite
a crowd. Do we have enough room in this
burrow? Do we have enough food?"

"Oh, dear," Mom said. "I thought we did, but
it looks as if we will be needing much more."

"Relax, Mom and Dad!" said Drake. "We
just need to shop today. I will make us a
shopping list in my notebook. It will be fine.
You'll see."

At the store, Drake reread his list out loud as they walked up and down rows.

"Uncle Dexter really likes Toasty Jelly Flakes," Mom said. "We will need many boxes of that brand of flakes for him. Does anyone else like them? How much should we get?"

Dad found a good deal on refried bangle beans. He dropped sixty cans into their cart.

Drake, Mom, and Dad returned home with a carful of food for the family. That was when they spotted the problem—a really BIG problem!

"Oh, no!" Dad exclaimed. "What is THAT?"

On the front stoop of their burrow lay a huge beast with a long, curly tail. It was sleeping soundly and blocking their way into the burrow.

"Did this really need to happen today?" Mom asked with a sigh.

"It's big, but harmless," Drake said. "It's a kind of hairy reptile called a snoreditch."

Dad marched over to the sleeping snoreditch.

"Please move," he said, but the beast did not seem to hear him. It just snored louder.

Dad tried to push the beast off the stoop, but it wouldn't budge. How would they ever get inside the burrow to prepare for their big family party?

Use That Word

Take turns. Play with a friend until you use all the words.

oh	sleep	family	today	enough
list	bed	shop	people	tomorrow

1. Pick a word and read it to your friend.

2. Your friend uses the word in a sentence.

3. Then your friend picks a word and reads it.

4. You use your friend's word in a sentence.

Blend and Read

1. unripe   retape   frozen   unsliced   unwisely

2. unlikely   recline   dislike   restate   compete

3. drifted   breezy   thrifty   scribble   squeeze

4. tallest   recalled   saltier   awfully   sawdust

5. unmute   graduated   organization

6. Drake and his family live in a remote place.

7. Today Drake wrote a list in his notebook.

8. Oh, dear! What is that huge reptile doing?

Party Time

by Bryan Langdo • illustrated by Karl West

Dad paced as he glared at the snoreditch sleeping peacefully on the stoop. It was completely blocking the way into the burrow and looked unlikely to wake up anytime soon.

"Hey, beast," Mom said as she gently poked the snoreditch. "This is not your bed! Please go find a better place to sleep. Hopefully, people are coming tomorrow, and we must prepare!"

"Maybe we can trick it with food," Drake said. He pulled a lime green dewmelly from the shopping bag at his feet. "This is the food snoreditches like best. Hopefully, this one will wake up and follow me to another spot."

Drake held up the dewmelly. Its sweet smell made the snoreditch sniff loudly a few times, but it did not come close to waking up.

As night fell, the snoreditch slept soundly on in front of the burrow.

"This is such an unlikely turn of events," Dad grumbled. "I suppose we'll be sleeping outside."

Drake, Mom, and Dad each found a place to sleep outside. Drake slept in his treehouse. Mom slept on a recliner. Dad slept on a table.

"This is hardly relaxing," said Mom. "Surely that beast will be gone by tomorrow."

Much to their surprise, the snoreditch was still
snoring peacefully on the stoop in the morning.

"Drake, do snoreditches hibernate?" Dad
asked. "If so, I fear this thing may be here for
much too long!"

Suddenly, they heard a loud voice. "We're
here!" Uncle Dexter called to them.

"I'm sad to say, the party is canceled," said
Mom, pointing at the cheerfully sleeping beast.

"Can't you just move it?" Uncle Dexter asked.

"Dad tried," Mom said, "but it weighs too much. Rethinking party plans is all we can do."

"Wait!" Drake cried. "The snoreditch does weigh a lot, but we have enough people to lift it."

With that, everyone surrounded the beast. They lifted it and lugged it carefully to a ditch far from the burrow.

"It will enjoy snoring in a ditch," said Drake.

Today is the day! It is party time now!

"You organized a nice party," said Uncle Dexter. "I'm glad we relocated that snoreditch!"

"Mom, Dad, I'm rethinking the layout of this burrow," said Drake. "I know all the family burrows on Planet Nine have just one way to get in—through the front. We need a new kind of burrow, with a way in through the back, too."

Uncle Dexter gave Drake a high five.

What If?

Reread both stories. Then write to answer the questions below.

1. What if the stories took place on Earth instead of Planet Nine? How might the stories be different?

2. What if a small reptile was sleeping on the front stoop instead of a huge one? How might the problem be different?

3. What if the burrow had a back door? How would that have changed the stories?

Share your answers with a group.

Get Started

What questions do you have about fossils? For example, how do fossils form? What can we learn by looking at fossils?

You will read about fossils and then about a boy named Gavin who goes hunting for fossils. Will he find any? Read to find out!

Traces of the Past

by Padma Bose

What IS that? That's the first question you might ask if you saw this object sticking out of a rock. It is a fossil. A fossil is a trace of life from a very long time ago that is preserved inside a rock. Fossils are like clues in a puzzle. They can help us discover what Earth was like long, long ago. Studying fossils is like taking a trip back in time.

Some fossils are bones and teeth. They were once parts of an animal. When this animal died, sand and mud covered its body. The soft body parts decayed quickly, but not the hard bones and teeth.

Over time, the sand and mud turned into rock. The bones and teeth changed, too. They turned into rock as well. That is how the fossils formed.

This is a fossil, too. It looks like a picture of a plant on a rock. When this plant died, it was covered with mud, and its shape was captured on this rock. That makes it what is called a trace fossil. The plant may be gone, but it left a trace of itself on the rock.

Experts can study a trace fossil to learn about plants long ago. It is like a picture and reveals details about the leaves and seeds of the plant.

© Roberto Nistri/Alamy

Footprints can be fossils, too. We can still see footprints that animals left in mud and sand long, long ago. We can measure the prints to find out how big the animals were. We can measure the spaces between the prints to find out about the motion of the animals and how fast they traveled. Isn't that cool?

Experts use tools to free fossils from the rocks that surround them. They need big tools, such as power drills, to extract big bones. They leave some rock around the fossil like a picture frame. This protects it and helps keep it in one piece.

Then the fossil is wrapped up in foam or plaster to keep it safe. Now it will travel to a lab where experts can study it and try to answer questions about the past.

In the lab, experts use tools to clean fossils. They use small chisels to pick at them and clear away bits of rock. They wear safety goggles when they cut and chip at the rock. They gently sweep away dust and dirt with little brushes.

Finally, the fossils are ready to display. People come from all over the world to gaze at fossils of huge reptiles and other animals from long, long ago.

Word Tally

Make a list of the words below.

animal	cut	inside	measure	pick
picture	rock	turned	question	where

1. Look for each word in the text. Make a tally mark each time you find a word.

2. Compare lists with a partner. Do your tallies match? Were any words missing?

3. Take turns with your partner. Use each word in a sentence.

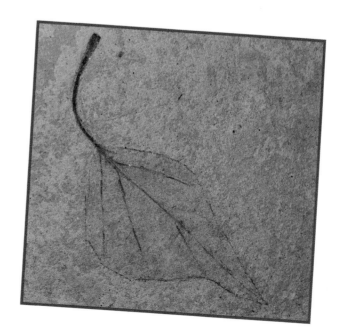

Blend and Read

1. fiction   topple   future   nature   puncture

2. unable   nation   mixture   texture   production

3. likely   reuse   mistake   unwise   disrespect

4. finite   mingle   unread   later   firelight

5. rubble   feeble   cultural   proportion

6. Use a brush to dust a portion of the fossil.

7. We found a bone from a little creature.

8. Hunting for fossils in rocks is an adventure.

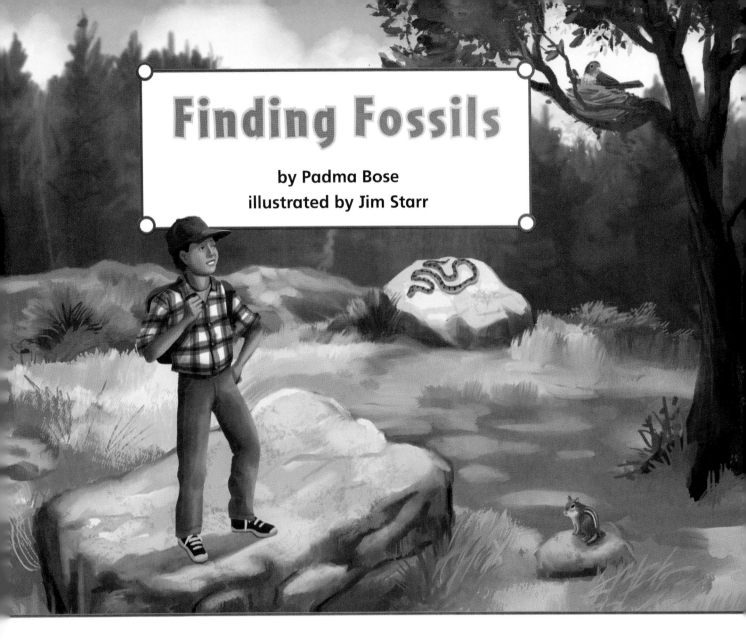

Finding Fossils

by Padma Bose
illustrated by Jim Starr

Gavin felt ready for adventure. He stood on a rock and gazed around him. He saw lots of small animals. Without even taking a single step, he could see chipmunks, a bird inside a nest, and a snake basking on a rock in the sun.

However, the kinds of creatures Gavin wanted to find today were inside the rocks. Today, Gavin was hunting for fossils.

"Where do we begin looking?" Gavin asked.

"Good question!" said Doc. "Doc" was a nickname for Doctor Hazel Cook. She was an old family friend. She was also a reptile expert and a fossil hunter.

Doc pointed to a section of the cliff. "See those rocks?" she said. "The ones that look like stacks of pancakes? That sort of rock often contains fossils."

Gavin walked over to the spot where Doc had pointed. He turned over some rocks and picked up others. As he hunted, he dreamed of what he might find.

He knew that fossil hunters had found many kinds of fossils where he lives. Seashells and sea creatures were common finds. So were ferns and plant parts such as leaves and pollen.

"Could we find an entire T. rex here, Doc?" asked Gavin.

"That's highly unlikely," said Doc. "But I helped dig up a T. rex skull once. We needed a small crane to lift it. We kept digging and found more T. rex bones in the area. Fossil bones can be scattered all over."

"It must be like doing a jigsaw puzzle to put them back together," said Gavin.

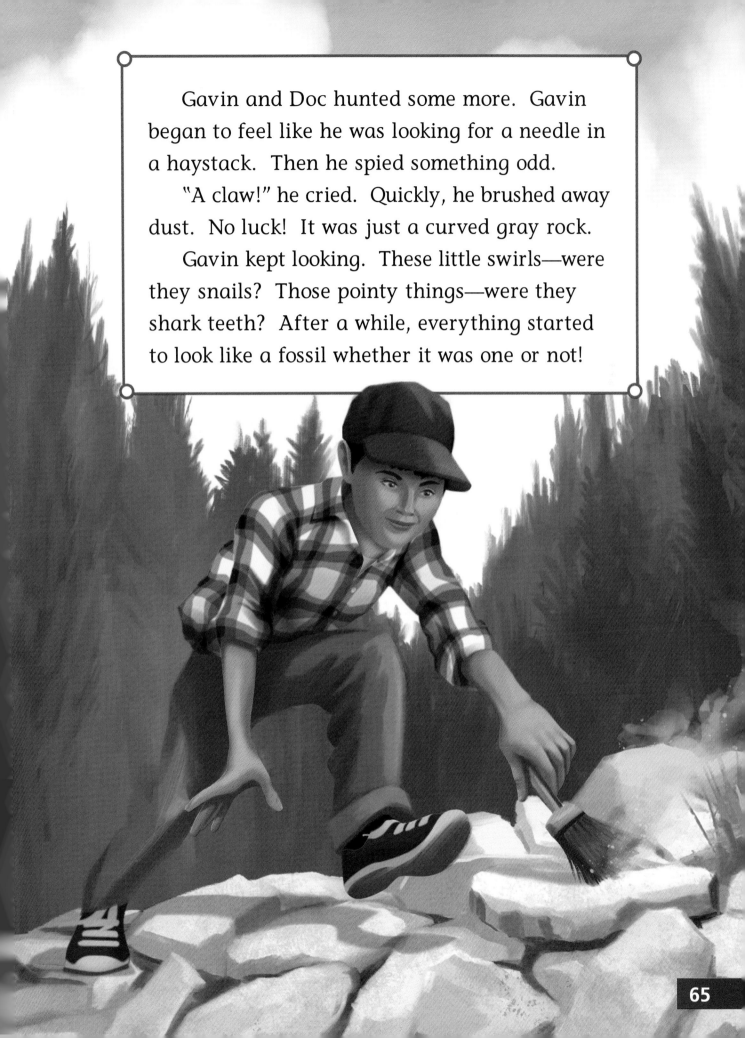

Gavin and Doc hunted some more. Gavin began to feel like he was looking for a needle in a haystack. Then he spied something odd.

"A claw!" he cried. Quickly, he brushed away dust. No luck! It was just a curved gray rock.

Gavin kept looking. These little swirls—were they snails? Those pointy things—were they shark teeth? After a while, everything started to look like a fossil whether it was one or not!

Then Gavin spotted something else. What were those lines in the rock? They looked like cuts made by a knife. The texture was bumpy.

"That's a chunk of mammoth tooth!" exclaimed Doc. "Cool find, Gavin! Let's take a picture, measure it, and record exactly where you found it. Then we can pick it out of the rock."

"Wow!" said Gavin. Maybe, just maybe, his next find would be a mammoth tusk!

Think-Draw-Pair-Share

Reread both texts. Think and then draw to answer these questions.

1. What are some different kinds of fossils? How do fossils form? Where can people find fossils?

2. How do experts remove fossils from rocks? What can they learn by studying a fossil?

3. Where does Gavin hunt for fossils? What kind of fossil does he find?

4. What kind of fossil would you like to find?

Share your work with a partner and then with a group.

Get Started

What do you know about moving to live in a new place?

Fergus is a boy who came to America from Ireland long ago. Kelly is a girl who lives in the present. She has a packet of old letters from her family in Ireland.

What do Fergus and Kelly have in common? What will Kelly find out from the letters? Read to find out!

Fergus

Kelly

America at Last

by Katherine Rawson | illustrated by William Owl

Fergus stood on the deck of the steamship, looking out at the wide blue sea. There was no land for as far as he could see.

It was breezy on deck, but Fergus liked to be out there to keep watch. He wanted to be the first person to see land. He could not wait to set eyes on his new homeland.

Fergus recalled things about his home in Ireland. He remembered his little stone house, the misty rain, the sheep, and the green hills.

Now his Uncle Pat lived in that house. Fergus and his family had left it behind forever. They were going to America. They would make a new home in a new country. It was not easy to say how Fergus felt about it. He felt happy and sad at the same time.

That night, Fergus sat at the dinner table with Mama, Papa, and his baby sister, Lizzie. Lizzie was wrapped up in a homemade blanket.

"When will we get to America?" Fergus asked. "It seems like years since we left home."

"We will be in New York soon," Mama said. She reached out and gave Fergus a hug. "In the meantime, let's think of this trip as an adventure at sea."

The next day, Fergus stood on the deck again. He gazed at the wide sea and smiled.

"I can't wait to get to America," he said to himself, "but that doesn't mean I can't try to enjoy being at sea."

He watched a gull sailing across the sky.

"Did you fly from New York?" Fergus asked the bird. Then his eyes grew wide as he spotted something far away.

It was Lady Liberty!

Fergus ran below to fetch Mama and Papa.

"We must be getting close to New York!" he cried. "Come up on the deck!"

Mama, Papa, and baby Lizzie followed Fergus to the deck. They watched the city loom larger as the ship moved closer to it.

"What a grand sight," said Papa. "We have reached America at last. The trip is complete."

Fergus pointed to the skyscrapers of New York City. "It is not like Ireland at all!" he said.

"Maybe not," Papa replied with a wink. "But I am sure we will grow to love America."

Fergus looked up at his mother. Her eyes were filled with tears.

"Mama, are you sad?" asked Fergus, puzzled.

"Just weeping with joy, Fergus my dear!" she said with a smile. "We have made it home."

Poetry Break

Read the poem with a partner.

Lady Liberty

As I write this **sentence**
The long trip is **complete**.
It wasn't **easy** to leave home
But life here will be sweet.

When we **reached America**—
I **can't** tell a lie—
Lady Liberty was **watching**
With **love** in her kind **eyes**.

And in that moment, I forgot
My worries and my fear.
Her gentle smile seemed to say,
"You are welcome here."

Tell your partner about a time when you moved to a new home, school, city, or **state**. How did you feel?

Blend and Read

1. habit   pickle   paper   noble   erase

2. inflate   flavor   denim   dribble   feline

3. corner   reflect   tornado   section   emotion

4. future   forever   feature   react   partner

5. populated   readmitted   possible

6. Fergus and his family left Ireland behind.

7. Lady Liberty welcomes people to America.

8. Fergus watched for land from the deck.

A Packet of Letters

by Katherine Rawson | illustrated by William Owl

Kelly glanced at the parcel on the table. Her eyes lit up as she read its label. "This came all the way from Ireland!" she said.

"This is from the family in Ireland," Mom told her. "I told them we were studying family history. Remember when we told you about your Great Uncle Fergus? He came to America when he was the same age as you are now. Inside this packet are some of his letters home."

Stuffed inside the parcel were old letters and other papers. "This is a complete surprise," said Mom. "I didn't know they'd send so much! I can't wait to read it all. This will really help us find out more about the family in the past."

Dad picked up a letter and began reading.

"Dear Uncle Pat," he read. "We have reached New York at last." Dad smiled. "Fergus wrote this one when he first got to America."

"What else does it say?" asked Kelly.

Dad cleared his throat and started reading again. "Papa began work at a market. He unloads boxes. Mama knows how to mend clothing, so she is working as a seamstress. They are glad to have jobs. We are careful with money, but at least we have enough to eat."

Kelly picked up another letter. She squinted at it. "The ink is really faded," she said. "It's not easy to read the first sentence."

"Try the next sentence," Dad said.

"Today I started school," read Kelly. "I made some friends in my class, and I learned that New York is not just a city. The state is called New York, too."

Kelly stopped reading and looked up. "Fergus is a bit like me," she said. "He started at a new school in America, and I started at a new school when we moved to this state last year."

"That was not an easy time for you," Mom said.

"Not at first," Kelly said, "but now I love my new school. I'm sure it was not easy for Fergus when he first moved here."

Kelly read the complete letter to Mom and
Dad. Then she returned it to the packet.

"This is so cool," Kelly said. "I can't wait to
read them all. May I keep this in my room?"

As she spoke, a little picture of Great Uncle
Fergus slipped out of the pile of letters. His
eyes seemed to twinkle at her.

"Hello, Great Uncle Fergus," said Kelly with
a grin. "It will be fun getting to know you!"

Show What You Know

Reread both stories. Use details from the stories to answer the questions.

1. What is the setting of each story? How are the settings the same? What is the biggest difference in the story settings?

2. Fergus and Kelly both move to a new home. How are their experiences similar? In what ways are they different?

3. How do Fergus and Kelly feel at different points in the stories? What do the words say? What is left unsaid?

Discuss your answers with a group.

Get Started

Do you know the folktale **The Three Billy Goats Gruff**? Like the goats in that story, three goats named Buttercup, Nettle, and Daisy are trying to get across a river to eat some yummy clover.

How will they get across the swift river? Who is Primrose? Read to find out!

Buttercup

Nettle

Daisy

The Three Goats

by Bryan Langdo • illustrated by Gediminas Pranckevičius

Three goats trotted down a dusty road. The biggest goat, Buttercup, led the way. Daisy, the smallest goat, was last. Nettle trotted between them in the middle.

Soon the goats came to a wide river that had a very swift current. The water swirled over and around sharp rocks. The goats could see grassy hills on the other side. Clover and other flowers grew wild on the slopes.

"That clover looks yummy," said Buttercup.

"I'm hungry," added Daisy. "I wouldn't mind eating a different kind of clover for a change."

"Shall we swim across?" asked Nettle. He stepped into the river and tried to swim, but the water was too cold. Nettle shivered. Buttercup and Daisy could hear his teeth chattering.

"This water is freezing!" he cried. He quickly leaped back onto the road.

Daisy tried swimming across next. "I don't mind the cold," she explained.

However, the fast current nearly swept Daisy right along with it as it raced downstream. She scrambled onto a big rock.

"I'm fine!" Daisy called. She retreated a few steps and leaped for shore. She sailed over the rapids and landed safely next to her pals.

"Well, that was a mistake!" Daisy said. "Can you swim across, Buttercup?"

Buttercup shook her head and grinned.

"No, but I have an idea," she said. "We can try doing something different. It's simple, really. For example, did you notice those wooden planks over there?"

Daisy laughed. "Good idea, Buttercup!"

Nettle giggled. "Silly us!"

The goats bounded toward the planks—and
that's when they heard a growly voice.

A creature lurked below them!

"Buttercup, yum," it mumbled. "Daisy.
Nettle. Oh, yum. It's almost time to eat, too."

Daisy gasped. "I don't know what that
creature is, but it seems to know who we are!"

"And its plan is to eat us!" Nettle said.

"Time to retreat!" cried Daisy.

"I'm not doing that," Buttercup said.

"Why not?" asked Nettle. "I don't mind. I'm prepared to forget all about eating clover. I think it's unwise to keep going. It's more important to stay safe than to eat different kinds of clover."

Buttercup did not reply. She was too busy thinking. Then, out of the blue, she bleated, "I have devised the perfect plan!"

Secret Word Game

 Play with a partner.
Use a timer. Take turns.

different	busy	doing	idea	I'm
important	mind	plan	next	tried

1. Think of a word in the box.

2. Set the timer.

3. Tell a clue about the word.

4. Your partner tries to guess the secret word.

5. Continue until your partner guesses or time runs out.

The first to guess five secret words wins!

Blend and Read

1. unused   meatier   mistaken   recklessly

2. untried   tireless   repaired   wakefulness

3. buttery   moping   mopping   opening

4. fixture   inspired   unsigned   creature

5. competition   interestingly   disinterested

6. Nettle disliked the freezing river water.

7. The goats are hungry for yummy clover.

8. Buttercup had a different and better idea.

The Creature

by Bryan Langdo • illustrated by Gediminas Pranckevičius

"Come closer, and I will tell you my plan,"
said Buttercup. Quietly, she whispered the plan
to her pals. Then she said, "Please remember,
it's important to keep in mind exactly what
to say as you cross." Daisy and Nettle winked
at her.

"I'll go first," declared Daisy, and she
stepped onto the planks.

Then a voice thundered, "Who goes there?"

Daisy gritted her teeth as a big creature popped its head out from under the planks.

"Please don't eat me!" Daisy squealed. "A different goat is on his way, and he is much bigger than I am. He will make a fine meal!"

With that, Daisy trotted across the planks. The creature scratched its head.

Next, Nettle stepped carefully onto the planks. The big creature peered at him.

Nettle tried to look as small as he could.

"Don't mind me," Nettle said. "I'm sure you are busy, and I don't want to disturb whatever you're doing. A much bigger goat will be on her way shortly. I'm sure you'll find her very filling."

With that, Nettle dashed off to join Daisy.

Then Buttercup stepped onto the planks. The creature held up a clawed paw. "Would you mind telling me what you goats think you're doing?" it said.

Buttercup gulped. She blinked her eyes rapidly. This was not part of her plan!

"We're just crossing the river to go and eat clover," she said. "By the way, a really big goat is just behind us. He will make a super meal!"

"I thought that might be the case," the creature said. "What I also want to know is this: why do you all want me to gobble up goats?"

"Don't you eat goats?" asked the goat.

The creature wrinkled its nose. "No way!" it replied. "I much prefer flowers. I've tried many different kinds. I love buttercups, daisies, nettles, clover, black-eyed Susans—you name it! If it's a flower, I eat it!"

Nettle and Daisy gasped when they spied
Buttercup romping toward them with the creature
right next to her. What was she doing?

"Nettle, Daisy, meet our new friend," Buttercup
called. "This is Primrose, and this lovely pasture is
her home and where she finds food to eat."

"Hello," said Primrose. "You will find some
uncommon and extremely yummy clover here! It's
great! Please join me. I'm hungry, too."

Think-Write-Pair-Share

Reread both stories. Think and then write answers to these questions.

1. How does knowing the story **The Three Billy Goats Gruff** help you understand these stories?

2. Why do the goats think that the creature under the planks wants to eat them?

3. Why is Primrose confused by what the goats say to her?

4. How does Primrose surprise the goats?

5. If you were Daisy, Nettle, or Buttercup, what would you say to Primrose? Explain.

Share your work with a partner and then in a group.

BOOK 1 **Missing Mama** p. 5

■ Decodable Words

TARGET SKILL: *Vowel Team Syllables*

eager, eating*, headed*, instead, Julie, peanut, replied, soaking, speedy, sweetest

PREVIOUSLY TAUGHT SKILLS

added, Alex, all*, and*, arm, asked*, at*, bad*, began*, better*, big*, bike, boy*, boys*, broke, broken, but*, can*, can't*, cast, chuckle, climbed, complete, cooked, cowboy, cried*, days*, did*, do*, each*, ended*, ever*, face, feels*, fell*, for*, forget, funny*, gentle, get*, gets*, go*, got*, grab, ground*, had*, hard*, he*, hear*, her*, his*, horse*, I*, I'm*, I've*, in*, it*, it's*, just*, kitchen, landed*, later, left*, let's*, like*, longer, look*, looked*, me*, miss*, most*, named*, Nan, nearly, never*, nice, no*, not*, off*, old*, on*, pancakes, picked*, pony, pop, puddle, quite, ride*, right*, saddle, sailed, see*, she*, shouted, side*, sitting*, smiling, started*, staying*, stopped*, story*, strutted, take*, taking*, tell*, ten, that*, that's*, them*, then*, things*, this*, time*, to*, told, too*, TV, until*, up*, Vincent, visit, wait*, we*, well*, wet, when*, while*, wide, wild, will*, with*, yay, years*, you*

■ High-Frequency Words
NEW

brother, happened, happy, help, home, mama, papa, sister, suddenly, surprise

PREVIOUSLY TAUGHT

a, about, across, again, ago, another, come, could, friend, friends, from, gone, have, laughing, many, of, other, said, school, some, the, their, two, was, were, what, who, work, you're, your

BOOK 2 **Papa Tells His Side** p. 13

■ Decodable Words

TARGET SKILLS: *Vowel Team Syllables; Multisyllabic Words*

agree, blueberry, coffeecake, downstairs, exclaimed, finally, greeted, Julie, peanut, really*, sideways, subway, sweetie

PREVIOUSLY TAUGHT SKILLS

afternoon, Alex, air*, all*, am*, an*, and*, arms, as*, ask*, asked*, at*, be*, bike, block, boys*, bronco, bucking, but*, came*, can*, carefully, cast, clinic, cried*, didn't*, do*, doing*, ended*, entered, fall*, fallen, fell*, flopped, flung, for*, funny*, giggled, go*, going*, good*, got*, grin, hands*, he*, hear*, her*, his*, house*, how*, hugged, I*, I'll*, I'm*, I've*, in*, inch, insisted, into*, is*, it*, it's*, leaped, letting*, like*, little*, look*, looked*, me*, mean, meet, miss*, much*, must*, my*, need*, nice, out*, named*, Nan, never*, no*, not*, now*, nudged, off*, old*, on*, onto, over*, pony, pop, referring, remember, rest, ride*, right*, say*, see*, she*, showed*, side*, smell, so*, soon*, standing, stay*, still*, stone, stop*, story*, take*, tell*, ten, thanks*, that*, them*, then*, they*, thing*, this*, tight, time*, to*, too*, town, told, train, true, up*, us*, used*, Vincent, visit, walk*, way*, we*, we'll*, we're*, well*, when*, wild, will*, winked, with*, won't*, write*, wrote, yelled, yes*, you*

■ High-Frequency Words
NEW

brother, happened, happy, help, home, mama, papa, sister, suddenly, surprise, surprised

PREVIOUSLY TAUGHT

a, across, anything, are, around, could, from, have, having, heard, here, laughed, moved, of, other, said, the, very, was, what, work, your

* = High-Frequency Word

BOOK 1 **Earth** p. 21

■ Decodable Words

TARGET SKILL: *r-Controlled Vowel Syllables*

before*, border, cooler, during, fairly, farmers, farther, forest, hardly, harvest, pattern, prefers, summer, summers, surrounds, survive, return, weather, wetter, winters

PREVIOUSLY TAUGHT SKILLS

all*, always*, and*, at*, be*, between, big*, bird*, blow, bottom, breezes, called*, can*, can't*, chilly, chunks, close*, coast, cold*, cool, corn, crops, day*, daytime, do*, dry, each*, eat*, end, enjoy, even*, fall*, far*, ferns, filled, find*, float, food*, for*, freezing, get*, globe, good*, grasslands, grow*, growing*, home*, hot*, ice, if*, in*, is*, it*, its*, jungles, land*, lands*, large, like*, likewise, little*, long*, look*, lots*, low, lush, may*, melt, middle, might*, more*, mostly, much*, near, north, not*, off*, on*, onto, or*, parts, place*, places*, planet, pole, poles, quite, reasons, repeats, rest, same*, seasons, see*, sheets, sky*, snow, snowy, so*, south, stay*, steamy, strong, tall, than*, that*, them*, then*, these*, they*, things*, third*, this*, thrive, time*, to*, too*, top, trees*, tropics, true, vines, we*, weak, well*, wet, wheat, while*, will*, with*, year*, you*, zone

■ High-Frequency Words
NEW

away, because, countries, country, earth, green, plant, rain, rains, rainy, sea, sun, sunlight

PREVIOUSLY TAUGHT

a, another, any, are, around, changes, covers, example, from, have, however, of, one, other, others, some, the, very, warm, water, your

---

BOOK 2 **Life on Earth** p. 29

■ Decodable Words

TARGET SKILLS: *r-Controlled Vowel Syllables; Multisyllabic Words*

Arctic, bigger, burrow, burrowing, butterflies, circle, darkens, darkness, flowering, flutter, furry, hardy, morsels, outer, over*, perfect, scamper, snowstorms, summer, surrounded, survive, winter

PREVIOUSLY TAUGHT SKILLS

air*, an*, and*, at*, be*, big*, bill, bird*, blend, blends, blow, branches, breezes, bright, but*, by*, called*, can*, cannot*, catch, chilly, close*, coat, cold*, cool, cozy, curl, day*, days*, desert, dirt, dives, drips, dry, each*, ears, eat*, eats*, eggs, entirely, far*, falls*, feathers, feet, few*, find*, fish*, flat, fluffy, fly*, food*, for*, form, fox, frogs, fur, fuzz, fuzzy, gets*, good*, grip, hare, has*, hawk, heat, help*, helps*, hidden, home*, hot*, hunting, ice, icy, in*, insects, into*, is*, it*, its*, keep*, keeps*, kind*, lands*, leafy, like*, make*, might*, much*, must*, nabs, nap, near*, need*, needs*, night*, north, not*, on*, onto, or*, out*, owl, paws, perch, place*, places*, pole, rocks*, sand, seem, skin, small*, snow, snowy, so*, south, spends, stay*, stiff, stops*, sweet, tail, take*, tan, than*, that*, these*, thick, thin*, this*, those*, to*, too*, tree*, trees*, tries*, tucked, turns*, until*, up*, vanish, walking*, wet, when*, whisks, white*, with*

■ High-Frequency Words
NEW

away, because, earth, else, green, plants, rain, rainforest, seas, sun

PREVIOUSLY TAUGHT

a, across, are, body, color, could, covering, discovered, does, doesn't, from, however, live, lives, many, mountain, of, pretty, the, very, warm, water, waterholes, waterproof, would

BOOK 1 **A Big Problem** p. 37

■ Decodable Words

TARGET SKILL: *Final* e *Syllables*

before*, beside, inside*, invite, notebook, prepare, rarely, remote, reptile, snoreditch

PREVIOUSLY TAUGHT SKILLS

and*, as*, asked*, at*, back*, bangle, be*, beans, beast, began*, big*, blocking, boxes, brand, budge, burrow, but*, called*, can*, cans*, carful, cart, crowd, curly, dad, day*, deal, dear, Dexter, did*, do*, down*, Drake, dropped, each*, event, ever, exclaimed, far*, felt*, fine, flakes, food*, for*, forth, found*, get*, good*, had*, hairy, happen*, happy*, harmless, he*, hear*, helped*, hill, him*, his*, home*, how*, huge, I*, if*, in*, into*, is*, it*, it's*, jelly, just*, kind*, last, lay, least, like*, likes*, long*, looks*, loud, louder, make*, marched, me*, members, mom, more*, much*, my*, need*, needing*, nine, no*, not*, off*, on*, out*, over*, party, planet, please*, problem, quite, ready*, really*, refried, relax, reread, returned*, room*, roomy, rows, saw*, say*, see*, seem, seen*, sigh, sixty, snored, so*, sooner*, soundly, spotted, stay*, stoop, store, tail, that*, them*, they*, this*, to*, toasty, told, too*, tried*, twenty, uncle, uncles, up*, us*, walked*, way*, we*, we'll*, we've*, weeks, when*, will*, wish*, with*, wow

■ High-Frequency Words
NEW

bed, enough, family, list, oh, people, shop, shopping, sleep, sleeping, today, tomorrow

PREVIOUSLY TAUGHT

a, anyone, away, does, early, else, front, have, here, lived, many, move, of, one, other, push, said, should, since, the, their, thought, very, was, what, would, wouldn't, you'll

BOOK 2 **Party Time** p. 45

■ Decodable Words

TARGET SKILLS: *Final* e *Syllables; Multisyllabic Words*

carefully, completely, hibernate, hopefully, organized, outside*, peacefully, prepare, recliner, relocated, snoreditch, snoreditches, snoring, suppose, surprise*, unlikely, waking

PREVIOUSLY TAUGHT SKILLS

all*, an*, and*, as*, asked*, at*, back*, bag, be*, beast, best*, better*, blocking, burrow, burrows, but*, by*, called*, can*, can't*, canceled, cheerfully, close*, cried*, dad, day*, dewmelly, Dexter, did*, ditch, do*, Drake, each*, enjoy, events, far*, fear, feet, fell*, few*, find*, five, follow, food*, for*, found*, gave*, gently, get*, glad, glared, go*, green*, grumbled, hardly, he*, held, hey, high*, his*, I*, I'm*, if*, in*, into*, is*, it*, its*, just*, kind*, know*, layout, lift, lifted, like*, lime, long*, looked*, lot, loud, loudly, lugged, made*, may*, maybe*, me*, mom, morning, much*, must*, need*, new*, nice, night*, nine, not*, now*, on*, paced, party, place*, planet, plans*, please*, pointing*, poked, relaxing, rethinking, sad, say*, she*, slept, smell, sniff, so*, soon*, soundly, spot, still, stoop, such*, suddenly, surrounded, sweet, table*, that*, them*, they*, thing*, this*, time*, times*, to*, today*, too*, treehouse, trick, tried*, turn*, uncle, up*, voice*, wake, wait*, way*, we*, we'll*, we're*, weigh, weighs, will*, with*, you*

■ High-Frequency Words
NEW

bed, enough, family, people, shopping, sleep, sleeping, tomorrow

PREVIOUSLY TAUGHT

a, another, anytime, are, come, coming, does, everyone, from, front, gone, have, heard, here, move, of, one, pulled, said, surely, through, the, their, through, was, your

BOOK 1 **Traces of the Past** p. 53

■ Decodable Words
TARGET SKILL: *Final Stable Syllables*
captured, goggles, little*, motion, puzzle

PREVIOUSLY TAUGHT SKILLS
all*, an*, and*, as*, ask*, at*, back*, be*, between, big*, bits, body*, bones, brushes, but*, called*, can*, changed, chip, chisels, clean*, clear, clues, cool, decayed, details, died, dirt, display, drills, dust, experts, extract, fast*, finally, find*, first*, foam, footprints, formed*, fossil, fossils, frame, free, gaze, gently, hard*, help*, how*, huge, if*, in*, into*, is*, isn't*, it*, its*, itself*, keep*, keeps*, lab, leave*, leaves*, left*, life*, like*, long*, looks*, makes*, may*, might*, mud, need*, not*, now*, object, on*, or*, out*, over*, parts, past, piece, plant*, plants*, plaster, power, preserved, prints, protects, quickly, ready, reptiles, reveals, safe, safety, sand, saw*, see*, seeds, shape, small*, soft, spaces, sticking, still, study*, studying*, such*, surround, sweep, taking*, teeth, that*, that's, them*, they*, this*, time*, to*, too*, tools, trace, travel, traveled, trip, try*, up*, us*, use*, we*, wear, well*, when*, will*, with*, wrapped, you*

■ High-Frequency Words
NEW
animal, animals, cut, inside, measure, pick, picture, question, questions, rock, rocks, turned, where

PREVIOUSLY TAUGHT
answer, are, around, away, come, covered, discover, earth, from, gone, learn, of, once, one, other, people, some, the, very, was, were, what, world

BOOK 2 **Finding Fossils** p. 61

■ Decodable Words
TARGET SKILLS: *Final Stable Syllables; Multisyllabic Words: Final Stable Syllables*
adventure, creatures, needle, puzzle, section, single, texture

PREVIOUSLY TAUGHT SKILLS
after*, all*, also*, an*, and*, as*, asked*, back*, basking, be*, began*, begin*, bird*, bones, brushed, bumpy, but*, by*, can*, chipmunks, chunk, claw, cliff, common, contains, cook, cool, crane, cried*, curved, dig, digging, do*, doc, doctor, doing*, dreamed, dust, entire, even*, exactly, exclaimed, expert, fell*, felt*, ferns, find*, finds*, for*, fossil, fossils, found*, Gavin, gazed, good*, gray, had*, haystack, hazel, he*, helped*, highly, him*, his*, hunted, hunter, hunters, hunting, I*, in*, it*, jigsaw, just*, kept*, kinds*, knew, knife, leaves*, lift, like*, lines*, little*, look*, looked*, looking*, lots, luck, made*, mammoth, maybe*, might*, more*, must*, needed*, nest, next*, nickname, no*, not*, odd, old*, on*, or*, out*, over*, pancakes, parts, plant*, pointed*, pointy, pollen, quickly, ready*, record, reptile, saw*, scattered, sea*, seashells, see*, shark, she*, skull, small*, snails, snake, so*, sort, spied, spot, spotted, stacks, started*, step, stood, such*, sun*, swirls, T. rex, take*, taking*, teeth, that*, that's*, them*, then*, these*, they*, things*, those*, to*, today*, tooth*, tusk, unlikely, up*, walked*, we*, whether, while*, without*, wow, you*

■ High-Frequency Words
NEW
animals, cuts, inside, measure, pick, picked, picture, question, rock, rocks, turned, where

PREVIOUSLY TAUGHT
a, area, around, away, could, else, everything, family, friend, here, however, let's, lives, many, of, often, once, one, ones, others, put, said, some, something, the, together, wanted, was, were, what, would

BOOK 1 **America at Last** p. 69

■ Decodable Words

TARGET SKILL: *Review of Syllable Types*

adventure, baby*, behind, being*, below, blanket, breezy, closer, dinner, enjoy, Fergus, followed*, forever, getting*, going*, happy*, himself*, homeland, homemade, Ireland, larger, lady, liberty, little*, Lizzie, looking, maybe*, meantime, misty, pointed*, puzzled, recalled, remembered, replied, sailing, sister*, skyscrapers, spotted, steamship, table*, uncle, weeping

PREVIOUSLY TAUGHT SKILLS

all*, am*, an*, and*, as*, asked*, at*, be*, bird*, blue*, but*, city*, close*, cried*, day*, dear, deck, did*, far*, felt*, fetch, filled, fly*, for*, gave*, gazed, get*, grand*, green*, grew*, grow*, gull, had*, he*, her*, hills, his*, home*, house*, how*, hug, I*, in*, is*, it*, joy, just*, keep*, land*, last, left*, let's*, like*, liked*, looked*, loom, made*, make*, mean, must*, my*, new*, next*, night*, no*, not*, now*, on*, out*, pat, rain*, ran*, sad, same*, sat*, say*, sea*, see*, seems, set*, she*, sheep, ship, sight, sky*, smile, smiled, soon*, stone, stood, tears, that*, then*, they*, things*, think*, this*, time*, to*, trip, try*, up*, wait*, we*, when*, wide, will*, wink, with*, wrapped, years*, York, you*

■ High-Frequency Words
NEW

America, can't, complete, easy, eyes, love, reached, watch, watched

PREVIOUSLY TAUGHT

a, about, across, again, are, away, come, could, country, doesn't, family, from, have, lived, mama, mother, moved, of, papa, said, since, something, sure, the, there, was, were, what, would

BOOK 2 **A Packet of Letters** p. 77

■ Decodable Words

TARGET SKILL: *Review of Syllable Types*

began*, boxes, careful, city*, clothing, faded, Fergus, getting*, hello*, history, inside*, Ireland, Kelly, label, letter*, letters*, market, packet, papers, parcel, picture*, reading*, really*, remember, returned, seamstress, squinted, started*, studying*, surprise*, table, today*, twinkle, uncle, unloads

PREVIOUSLY TAUGHT SKILLS

age, all*, an*, and*, as*, asked*, at*, be*, bit, but*, called*, came*, class, cleared, cool, dad, dear, didn't*, eat*, find*, first*, for*, fun*, glad, glanced, got*, grin, he*, help*, her*, his*, home*, how*, I*, I'm*, in*, ink, is*, it*, its*, jobs, just*, keep*, know*, knows*, last, least, like*, lit, little*, looked*, made*, mail, may*, me*, mend, more*, much*, my*, new*, next*, not*, now*, old*, on*, out*, past, pat, picked*, pile, read*, room*, same*, say*, seemed, send, she*, slipped, smiled, so*, spoke, stopped*, stuffed, that*, them*, they*, they'd, this*, throat, time*, to*, told, too*, try*, up*, us*, wait*, way*, we*, when*, will*, with*, wrote, year*, York, you*

■ High-Frequency Words
NEW

America, can't, complete, easy, eyes, love, reached, sentence, state

PREVIOUSLY TAUGHT

a, about, another, are, does, else, enough, family, friends, from, great, have, here, learned, mama, money, moved, of, one, other, papa, said, school, some, sure, the, was, were, what, work, working, your

BOOK 1 **The Three Goats** p. 85

■ Decodable Words

TARGET SKILL: *Review Affixes*

added, asked*, biggest, bleated, bounded, called*, chattering*, creature, devised, dusty, eating*, explained, flowers, freezing, gasped, giggled, grassy, growly, hungry, landed*, leaped, lurked, mistake, mumbled, nearly, prepared, quickly, really*, reply, retreat, retreated, safely, sailed, scrambled, shivered, smallest, stepped, swimming, swirled, thinking*, trotted, unwise, yummy

PREVIOUSLY TAUGHT SKILLS

all*, almost*, an*, and*, as*, back*, below*, between, big*, blue*, but*, buttercup, came*, can*, clover, cold*, cried*, current, daisy, did*, don't*, down*, downstream, eat*, fast*, few*, fine, for*, forget, goat, goats, going*, good*, grew*, grinned, had*, he*, head*, hear*, her*, hills, his*, I*, in*, into*, is*, it*, it's*, its*, keep*, kind*, kinds*, know*, last, led, looks*, middle, more*, nettle, no*, not*, on*, onto, out,* over*, pals, perfect, planks, raced, rapids, right*, river*, road, rock*, rocks*, safe, see*, seems, shall*, sharp, she*, shook, shore, side*, silly, simple, slopes, soon*, stay*, steps, swept, swift, swim, teeth, than*, that*, that's, them*, then*, they*, think*, this*, those*, three*, time*, to*, too*, try*, us*, voice*, way*, we*, well*, when*, why*, wide, wild, with*, wooden, you*, yum

■ High-Frequency Words

NEW

busy, different, doing, I'm, idea, important, mind, next, plan, tried

PREVIOUSLY TAUGHT

a, about, across, along, are, around, change, could, example, have, heard, however, laughed, notice, of, oh, other, said, should, something, the, there, toward, very, was, water, what, who, wouldn't

BOOK 2 **The Creature** p. 93

■ Decodable Words

TARGET SKILL: *Review Affixes*

asked*, bigger, blinked, called*, carefully, clawed, closer, creature, crossing, daisies, dashed, declared, disturb, exactly, extremely, filling, gasped, gritted, gulped, hungry, peered, popped, quietly, rapidly, really*, remember, replied, romping, scratched, shortly, spied, squealed, stepped, telling*, thundered, trotted, uncommon, whispered, winked, wrinkled, yummy

PREVIOUSLY TAUGHT SKILLS

all*, also*, am*, and*, as*, at*, be*, behind, big*, black, buttercup, buttercups, by*, case, clover, cross, daisy, do*, don't*, eat*, find*, finds*, fine, first*, flower, flowers, food*, go*, goat, goats, gobble, he*, head*, held*, hello*, her*, him*, his*, home*, I*, I'll*, I've*, if*, in*, is*, it*, it's*, its*, join*, just*, keep*, kinds*, know*, look*, make*, me*, meal, meet, might*, much*, my*, name*, nettle, nettles, new*, no*, nose, not*, off*, on*, onto, out*, pals, part, pasture, paw, planks, please*, prefer, primrose, right*, river*, say*, she*, small*, super, Susans, teeth, tell*, than*, that*, them*, then*, they*, think*, this*, to*, too*, under*, up*, us*, voice*, way*, we're*, when*, why*, will*, with*, you*

■ High-Frequency Words

NEW

busy, different, doing, I'm, important, mind, next, plan, tried

PREVIOUSLY TAUGHT

a, across, are, eyed, come, could, eyes, friend, from, goes, great, here, love, lovely, many, of, our, said, some, sure, the, there, thought, toward, very, want, was, what, whatever, where, who, would, you'll, you're